19.95

Countries We Come From

Jamaica

by Jessica Rudolph

Consultant: Karla Ruiz
Teacher's College, Columbia University
New York, New York

BEARPORT
PUBLISHING

New York, New York

Credits

Cover, © Nolte Lourens/Shutterstock and jlvphoto/iStock; 3, © Royliem26/Dreamstime; 4, © Kkulikov/Shutterstock; 5T, © irabel8/Shutterstock; 5B, © Yevgen Belich/Shutterstock; 7, © jiawangkun/Shutterstock; 8, © KKulikov/Shutterstock; 9T, © Konstik/iStock; 9B, © Pakhnyushchy/Shutterstock; 10T, © Rod Williams/Nature Picture Library; 10B, © 33karen33/iStock; 11T, © Leena Robinson/Shutterstock; 11B, © Rolf Nussbaumer Photography/Alamy Stock Photo; 12, © akg-images/Newscom; 13, © FORGET Patrick/SAGAPHOTO/Alamy Stock Photo; 14, © Dorling Kindersley Ltd/Alamy Stock Photo; 15, © Rawpixel.com/Shutterstock; 16, © Juanmonino/iStock; 17, © Michael Dwyer/Alamy Stock Photo; 18, © Michael Dwyer/Alamy Stock Photo; 18B, © FLPA/Alamy Stock Photo; 19T, © bonchan/Shutterstock; 19B, © Maks Narodenko/Shutterstock; 20, © Shane Luitjens/Alamy Stock Photo; 21, © imageBROKER/Alamy Stock Photo; 22–23, © Peeter Viisimaa/iStock; 23B, © robertharding/Alamy Stock Photo; 24, © Dario Sabljak/Shutterstock; 25, © Pictorial Press Ltd/Alamy Stock Photo; 26–27, © DebbiSmirnoff/iStock; 26B, © Paul_Brighton/Shutterstock; 28T, © Jeffrey Boan/AP Images; 28B, © Swapan Photography/Shutterstock; 29, © David Alayo/Dreamstime; 30T, © Halima_Halima/iStock and © Anton_Ivanov/Shutterstock; 30B, © PCN Photography/Alamy Stock Photo; 31(T to B), © Peeter Viisimaa/iStock, © Ozphotoguy/Shutterstock, © Everett Historical/Shutterstock, © KKulikov/Shutterstock, and © Paul Springett C/Alamy Stock Photo; 32, © catwalker/Shutterstock.

Publisher: Kenn Goin
Editor: J. Clark
Creative Director: Spencer Brinker
Design: Debrah Kaiser
Photo Researcher: Olympia Shannon

Library of Congress Cataloging-in-Publication Data

Names: Rudolph, Jessica, author.
Title: Jamaica / by Jessica Rudolph.
Description: New York, New York : Bearport Publishing, [2017] | Series:
    Countries we come from | Includes bibliographical references and index. |
    Audience: Ages 6–10.
Identifiers: LCCN 2016007663 (print) | LCCN 2016008037 (ebook) | ISBN
    9781944102722 (library binding) | ISBN 9781944102913 (ebook)
Subjects: LCSH: Jamaica—Juvenile literature.
Classification: LCC F1872.2 .R (print) | LCC F1872.2 (ebook) | DDC
    972.92—dc23
LC record available at http://lccn.loc.gov/2016007663

For more information, write to Bearport Publishing Company, Inc., 45 West 21st Street, Suite 3B, New York, New York 10010. Printed in the United States of America.

10 9 8 7 6 5 4 3 2 1

Contents

This Is Jamaica

Beautiful

Colorful

MUSICAL

Jamaica is an island country.
It's located in the Caribbean Sea.
Almost three million people live there.

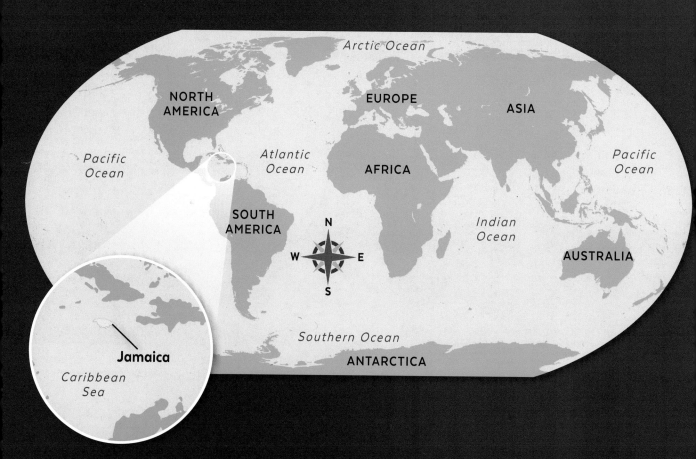

Jamaica is a **tropical** nation. It's warm all year.

Jamaica has different kinds of land.

There are sandy beaches along the coast.

Tall mountains cover much of the island.

Jamaica also has swamps with mangrove trees. The trees' long roots grow in the water.

Many amazing animals live in Jamaica.

Jamaican boas slither in trees.

Manatees swim in rivers.

Giant swallowtails flutter around.

The streamertail hummingbird is Jamaica's national bird. Its tail is twice as long as its body!

The Taíno (TYE-noh) were the first people to live in Jamaica.

In 1494, the Spanish arrived and began to rule the island.

Then, in 1655, the English took over.

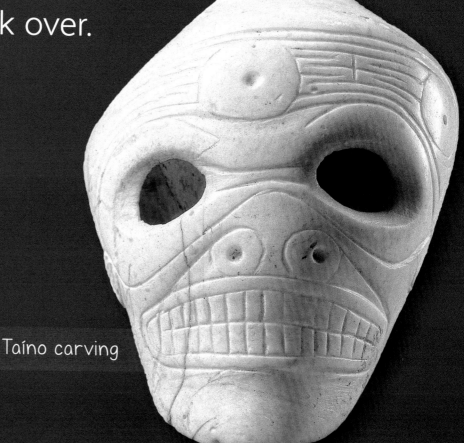

Taíno carving

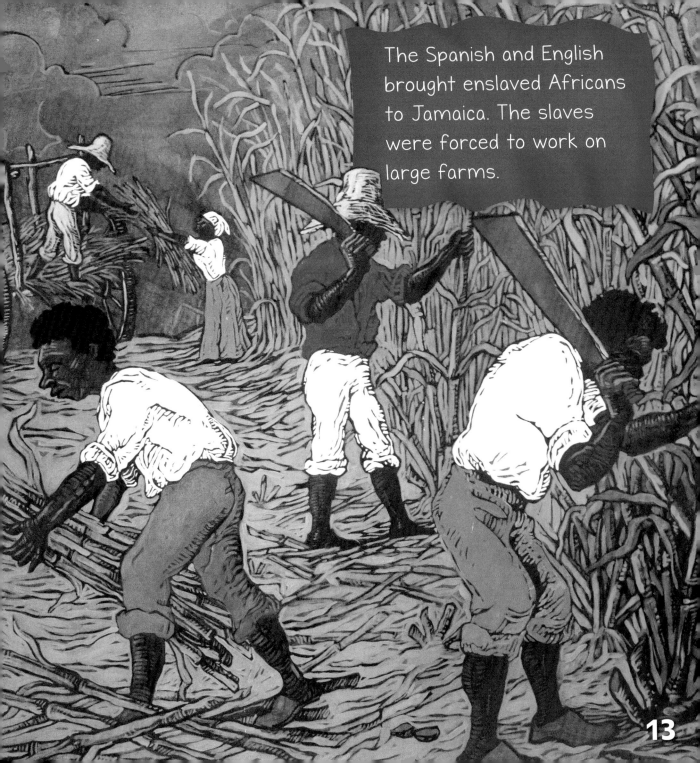

The Spanish and English brought enslaved Africans to Jamaica. The slaves were forced to work on large farms.

Enslaved people were treated very poorly.

Some slaves led **revolts** to fight for their freedom.

In 1838, slavery was outlawed.

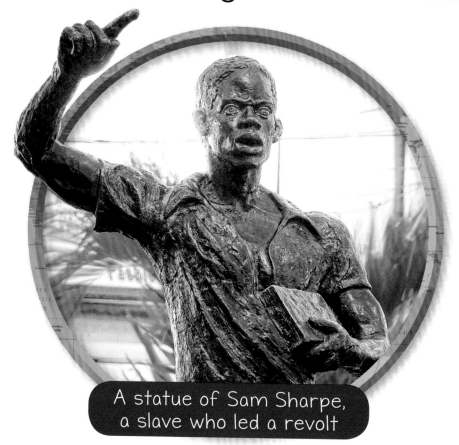

A statue of Sam Sharpe, a slave who led a revolt

Jamaica became free from English rule in 1962.

Most Jamaicans speak English and Patois (PA-twah).

This is how you say *hello* in Jamaican Patois:

Yao (YOW)

Jamaican Patois is a mix of words from English and African languages.

This is how you say *what's going on*:

Wha' gwan (WUH GWAHN)

Jamaicans have many kinds of jobs.

Some people work on farms.

They raise goats and cows.

Farmers also grow foods like yams and bananas.

19

Many Jamaicans work in **tourism**.

Some have jobs at restaurants and hotels.

Others are **tour guides** for divers and hikers.

About two million people visit Jamaica each year!

Kingston is the nation's **capital**.

It's also the country's largest city.

About one–third of all Jamaicans live in Kingston.

Jamaica is famous for reggae (REG-ay) music.

Reggae has a bouncy beat.

It's played with drums, guitars, and other instruments.

Bob Marley was a Jamaican reggae musician. People all over the world listen to his songs.

Jamaicans make tasty meals like jerk chicken.

The chicken is covered with spices.

Then it's cooked over a fire.

Many Jamaicans eat saltfish and ackee. Ackee is a fruit. It looks like scrambled eggs when it's cooked.

jerk chicken

What do Jamaicans like to do for fun? Play sports!

Cricket is very popular.

This game is similar to baseball.

cricket ball

Soccer is also played all over the country. In Jamaica, soccer is called football.

Fast Facts

Capital city: Kingston

Population of Jamaica: Almost three million

Main language: English

Money: Jamaican dollar

Major religion: Christianity

Nearby countries include: Cuba, Haiti, and the Dominican Republic

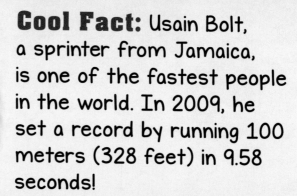

Cool Fact: Usain Bolt, a sprinter from Jamaica, is one of the fastest people in the world. In 2009, he set a record by running 100 meters (328 feet) in 9.58 seconds!

capital (KAP-uh-tuhl) a city where a country's government is based

revolts (ri-VOHLTS) uprisings; fights against authority

tour guides (TOOR GIDEZ) people who take others on trips and explain interesting details about an area

tourism (TOOR-iz-uhm) the practice of traveling to places for fun

tropical (TROP-i-kuhl) having to do with the warm areas of Earth near the equator

Index

Read More

Coster, Patience. *My Life in Jamaica (Children of the World).* New York: Cavendish Square (2015).

Green, Jen. *Jamaica (Countries of the World).* Washington, DC: National Geographic (2008).

Learn More Online

To learn more about Jamaica, visit
www.bearportpublishing.com/CountriesWeComeFrom

About the Author

Jessica Rudolph lives in Connecticut. She has edited and written many books about history, science, and nature for children.